25 Read & Write Mini-Books

That Teach Word Families

BY NANCY I. SANDERS

SCHOLASTIC
PROFESSIONAL BOOKS

NEW YORK • TORONTO • LONDON • AUCKLAND • SYDNEY
MEXICO CITY • NEW DELHI • HONG KONG

I dedicate this book to my family:

my husband Jeff,

and our sons Dan, age 16,

and Ben, age 14.

May you always enjoy reading!

Cover design by Susan Kass
Interior design by Kathy Massaro
Cover and interior art by Anne Kennedy

ISBN 0-439-15587-8
Copyright © 2001 by Scholastic Inc.
Printed in U.S.A.

Contents

About This Book

What makes a good reader? Research shows that strong readers are able to decode new words through analogy to known words rather than by sounding them out letter by letter. "The best differentiator between good and poor readers is repeatedly found to be their knowledge of spelling patterns and their proficiency with spelling-sound translations." (from *Beginning to Read: Thinking and Learning About Print* by M. Adams; MIT Press,1990) Teaching with phonograms, also called *word families* and *chunks*, is a highly effective way to help young children acquire and implement these kinds of reading skills and strategies.

Phonograms are recognizable chunks of letters that appear with regularity in words. For example, the words *quack, stack, rack, back,* and *Jack* all share the phonogram *-ack*. When children learn the sound and spelling of chunks such as *-ack*, they can decode by analogy—that is, apply what they know to new words they encounter. So, for example, instead of struggling to sound out the word *pack* one letter at a time (and then blending the letters to come up with a recognizable word), a child can more quickly and efficiently decode the word by putting two familiar sounds together—the sound for *p* and the sound for *-ack*. Multiply this success by the many words that can be generated by a small number of phonograms and the result is a more efficient (and happy) reader!

25 Read & Write Mini-Books That Teach Word Families is designed to support instruction in the spelling patterns and letter-sound correspondence that will help your students build these essential reading skills. Each of the 25 reproducible word family mini-books features a key phonogram in a simple one-sentence story. As children follow each story's predictable pattern of rhyming words, they'll gain confidence as readers. Fluency will follow, as children apply what they learn to recognize hundreds of words in the same families. The size of these easy-to-make mini-books adds to their appeal—they're just the right size for small hands and easily tucked into a pocket to take anywhere.

Making the Mini-Books

Follow these steps to copy and put together the mini-books.

☼ Remove the mini-book pages along the perforated lines. Make a double-sided copy on 8 1/2- by 11-inch paper.

Page 5	Page 4
Page 8	Title Page

← Page 2

☼ Cut the page in half along the solid line. ✂

Page 5	Page 4
Page 8	Title Page

☀ Place page 3 behind the title page.

Page 6	Page 3
Page 8	Title Page

☀ Fold the pages in half along the dotted line. Check to be sure that the pages are in the proper order, and then staple them together along the book's spine.

NOTE: If you do not wish to make double-sided copies, you can photocopy single-sided copies of each page, cut apart the mini-pages, and stack them together in order, with the title page on top. Staple the pages together along the left-hand side.

Using the Mini-Books

The mini-books in this collection will spark the interest and enthusiasm of your students, each one inspiring them to read another! Each mini-book tells a humorous one-sentence story that incorporates four key words from the same word family. The books follow the same format and include illustrations to support young readers.

☀ The title page introduces children to the first word from the word family—for example, *Jack*.

☀ Pages 2 and 3 introduce the second key word in the sentence.

Readers see the word divided into the *onset* (*p*) and the word family or *rime* (*-ack*). Children can practice writing the word by tracing over the dotted lines of the onset letters.

☀ Pages 4 and 5 add on to the story, introducing and reinforcing a third key word (*back*).

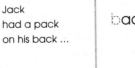

☀ Pages 6 and 7 introduce and reinforce the fourth key word

(*quack*), and the story is completed.

☀ Children can revisit the four key words on the back cover of each book by filling in the missing letters in the onsets to reinforce spelling.

Activities to Extend Learning

Pocket Chart Phonics

Before students make a mini-book, use this pocket chart activity to introduce the word family.

☀ Write the featured phonogram 10 to 12 times on sturdy paper. Cut apart to make phonogram cards.

☀ Write individual alphabet letters, blends, and digraphs on sturdy paper. Cut apart to make letter cards. (Make them about the same height as the phonogram cards.)

☀ Place the phonogram cards in the pocket chart. One at a time, hold up different alphabet letters, blends, and digraphs. Ask: *Can we put this letter /these letters at the beginning of these letters (the phonogram) to make a word?* Encourage students to sound out the onset and rime as they determine their answers.

☀ As children form each new word, display it on the pocket chart. Review the words students form, reading them aloud as a class and letting children take turns reading them independently.

Backpack Phonics

Write a word family, such as *-at*, on a sheet of construction paper. Show the paper to students. Brainstorm words that contain this word family, such as *cat, bat,* and *mat*. Ask each child to choose a word to illustrate. Help them label their pictures with the correct spelling of the corresponding words. Place all of the pictures in a backpack along with the paper on which you wrote the word family. Display the backpack in a place where students can use it during the week. Have them "unpack" it, looking at the pictures and reading the words. Repeat the activity with new word families to give children several backpacks from which to choose. Once you've introduced the mini-book that goes with each backpack, add a copy to the backpack.

Word Family Murals

Children can add to these colorful, print-rich murals as they wish, learning new words each time. Write a phonogram in large letters on a mural-sized sheet of craft paper. Write a word from that word family on the paper and illustrate it. Display the mural in a place where children will have easy access to it. Invite them to add words in the same word family and illustrate them. (Children can draw pictures or cut them out of magazines.) You can have several of these word family murals going at once, giving children lots of opportunities to reinforce their reading and spelling skills.

Take Your Corner!

Choose four phonograms to focus on and write each one on a sheet of paper. Display one phonogram sign in each corner of the room. Write words that belong in each of those word families on index cards. Be sure you have a class set. Mix up the cards and give one to each child. Tell children that when they hear the sound that is the same as a sound in their word, they should hold up their card above their head. The first child to hold up the card stands up and goes to that word family corner. Say the sound for one of the phonograms, and have the child who holds up his or her card first go to the appropriate corner. Continue, saying the phonogram sounds at random, until every child is standing in a corner. Let children exchange word cards and play again.

Word Family Activity Cards

Make multiple copies of the word cards on pages 8–14. (These are the 100 words introduced in the mini-books.) Cut them apart and use them for a variety of activities. Suggestions follow.

☼ Collaborative Easy Reader

Divide the class into groups of four students each. Cut apart the word cards and give each group a set (the four key words from the mini-book). Have children glue each word to a sheet of paper, then find pictures to go with the words and paste them on the papers. (They can also draw pictures to go with the words.) When they are finished, have children work together to arrange the illustrated pages by word families. Add a cover and put the pages together to make an easy-reader book.

☼ Word Family Flash Cards

Cut apart the word cards and glue each to an index card. Glue or draw a picture on the back. Place the word family cards for each phonogram in an envelope and label it. Let children use the flash cards with partners. One student holds up the first flash card and shows the printed word to his or her partner, who reads the word. Children can use the pictures on the backs of the cards to self-check.

☼ Move and Match

Glue each word card to a sheet of colorful paper. For more fun, cut the paper into shapes first, such as stars. Have children sit at their desks or tables, put their heads down, close their eyes, and hold their hands out. Place a word card in each child's hand. When everyone has a word card, invite children to open their eyes and stand up. Have them move about, looking for classmates with matching word family cards. Have children sit down with their matching classmates when they think they have found them all. Let children take turns reading their words aloud. Invite classmates to suggest new words that go with each word family.

snail

quail

☼ Concentration

Cut apart the word cards and glue them to index cards. (Or use the word family flash cards for this activity. See page 8.) Choose five or six sets of cards for this game. Mix up the cards and place them facedown on a table or the floor. Have one child turn over two cards. If they have a matching phonogram, this player keeps the cards. If not, the cards are placed facedown again and the next player takes a turn. Play continues until each match is made. (With four words for each phonogram, children can make two matches per word family.)

☼ Silly Sentence Makers

Cut apart the word cards and place them in a basket. Let children take turns selecting a word at random and saying a sentence that uses both that word and a word with the same phonogram. For example, if a child selects the word *chick*, he or she might say, *The chick gave my ice cream cone a lick.*

☼ "I Can Read" Word Rings

Give each child a set of word-card pages and an O-ring. Have children cut apart the words, one word family at a time. When children can read each of the key words in a word family, have them punch a hole in the left corner of each card and put it on the O-ring. Children's O-rings will grow quickly as they learn all 100 words in the mini-books. Take time to meet with a few children each day to let them read their words to you. (This will take only a minute or two per child but will help build confidence and feelings of success in your young readers.) Then encourage children to take their O-rings home to share with their families.

Word Cards

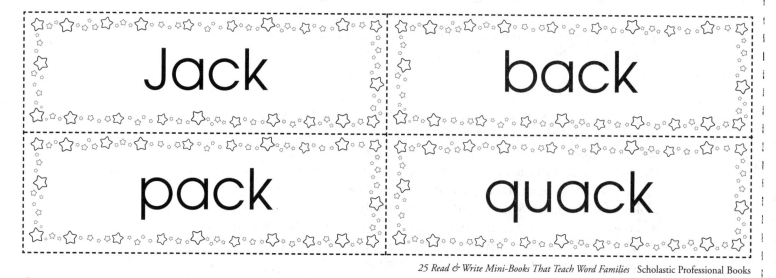

snail	Dale
quail	bale
mail	whale
pail	scale
snake	shark
bake	Mark
cake	park
lake	dark

cat	sheep
rat	jeep
hat	beep
bat	sleep
Kate	shell
plate	spell
gate	bell
skate	well

25 Read & Write Mini-Books That Teach Word Families Scholastic Professional Books

Ben	mice
pen	dice
hen	rice
ten	ice
pet	chick
jet	trick
vet	brick
wet	stick

bride	knight
hide	light
ride	night
slide	fright
pig	Bill
wig	Jill
big	hill
dig	mill

25 Read & Write Mini-Books That Teach Word Families Scholastic Professional Books

king	frog
ring	dog
sing	jog
swing	log
peacock	cop
rock	stop
clock	top
tock	mop

cub	bug
sub	rug
scrub	mug
tub	hug
duck	skunk
buck	trunk
truck	bunk
stuck	junk

25 Read & Write Mini-Books That Teach Word Families Scholastic Professional Books

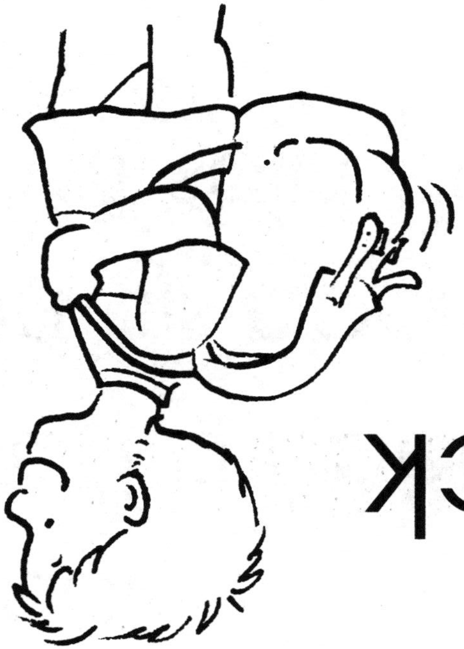

Jack
had a pack
on his back ...

Jack

back

ack

ack

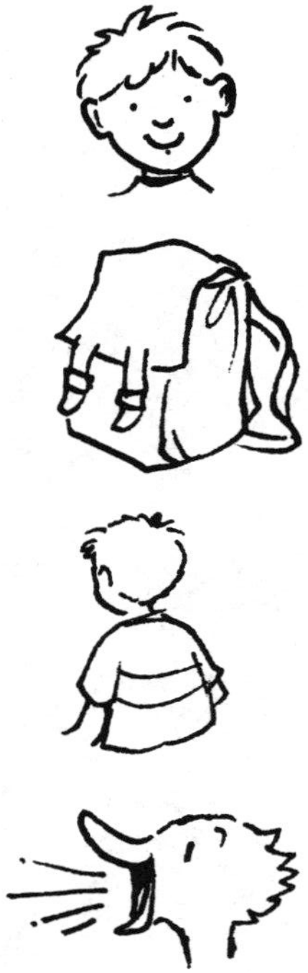

ack

____ ack

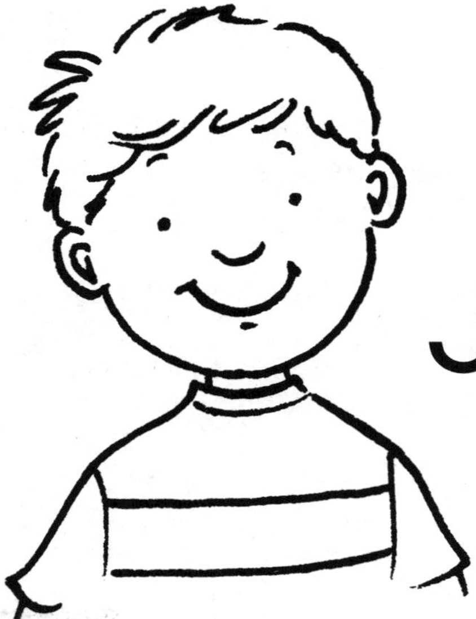

3

p͟ack

2

Jack
had a pack ...

25 Read & Write Mini-Books That Teach Word Families Scholastic Professional Books

6

Jack
had a pack
on his back
that said quack!

7

q͟uack

A snail
and a quail
get some mail ...

A Snail

mail

ai_
ai_
ai_
ai_

25 Read & Write Mini-Books That Teach Word Families Scholastic Professional Books

3

quail

2

A snail
and a quail ...

6

A snail
and a quail
get some mail
in a pail.

7

pail

Dale
put a bale
on the whale ...

Dale

whale

5

__ale

__ale

__ale

__ale

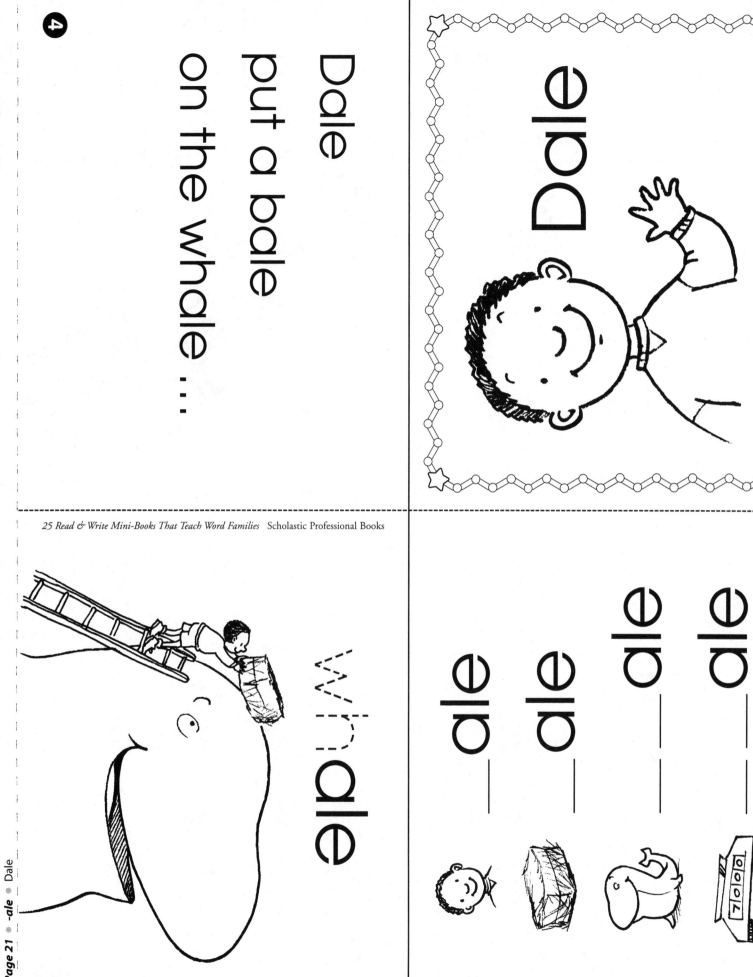

3

bale

2

Dale
put a bale ...

6

Dale
put a bale
on the whale
on a scale.

7

scale

4

The shark
played with Mark
at the park ...

The Shark

5

p ark

8

___ ark

___ ark

___ ark

___ ark

2

The shark
played with Mark ...

3

Mark

7

Clark

6

The shark
played with Mark
at the park
until dark.

Kate
tries a plate
through the gate ...

Kate

25 Read & Write Mini-Books That Teach Word Families Scholastic Professional Books

＿ate

5

ate

＿ate

＿ate

＿ate

A snake
_ake
Page 19

8

plate

3

Kate
takes a plate ...

2

Kate
takes a plate
through the gate
on a skate.

6

skate

7

The Sheep

The sheep
drove the jeep
and went beep ...

_ eep

eep

eep

eep

eep

25 Read & Write Mini-Books That Teach Word Families   Scholastic Professional Books

4

5

8

The sheep
drove the jeep ...

jeep

Scholastic Professional Books

sleep

The sheep
drove the jeep
and went beep
in his sleep.

The shell
likes to spell
and ring the bell ...

The Shell

25 Read & Write Mini-Books That Teach Word Families Scholastic Professional Books

S·H·E·L·L
spells shell.

b e l l

__ ell

__ ell

__ ell

__ ell

S·H·E·L·L
spells shell.

The shell
likes to spell ...

spell

S·H·E·L·L
spells shell

well

S·H·E·L·L
spells shell.

The shell
likes to spell
and ring the bell
at the well.

Ben
in the pen
with the hen ...

Ben

25 Read & Write Mini-Books That Teach Word Families   Scholastic Professional Books

hen

en
en
en
en

10

2

Ben
in the pen ...

3

pen

7

ten

6

Ben
in the pen
with the hen
counts to ten.

My pet
rode a jet
to the vet ...

My
Pet

25 Read & Write Mini-Books That Teach Word Families Scholastic Professional Books

vet

__et

__et

__et

__et

3

jet

2

My pet
rode a jet ...

25 Read & Write Mini-Books That Teach Word Families Scholastic Professional Books

6

My pet
rode a jet
to the vet
and got wet.

7

wet

4

The mice
played with dice
and ate rice ...

The Mice

25 Read & Write Mini-Books That Teach Word Families Scholastic Professional Books

r ice

5

ice

ice

ice

ice

8

The mice
played with dice ...

dice

The mice
played with dice
and ate rice
on the ice.

ice

The chick
did a trick
with a brick ...

The Chick

4

b r ick

ick ___

ick ___

ick ___

ick ___

25 Read & Write Mini-Books That Teach Word Families   Scholastic Professional Books

5

8

The chick
did a trick ...

trick

stick

The chick
did a trick
with a brick
on a stick.

4

The bride
likes to hide
and ride ...

The
Bride

___ide

5

ide

ide

ide

ide

8

The bride
likes to hide ...

hide

slide

The bride
likes to hide
and ride
down the slide.

A pig
in a wig
who is big ...

A Pig

25 Read & Write Mini-Books That Teach Word Families   Scholastic Professional Books

big

b i g

_ig

_ig

_ig

_ig

A pig
in a wig ...

wig

dig

A pig
in a wig
who is big
likes to dig.

4

The knight
with the light
in the night ...

The Knight

25 Read & Write Mini-Books That Teach Word Families   Scholastic Professional Books

5

The night

8

ight ———
ight ———
ight ———
ight ———

3

ight

2

The knight
with the light ...

6

The knight
with the light
in the night
had a fright.

7

fr ight

Bill
and Jill
went up the hill ...

Bill

25 Read & Write Mini-Books That Teach Word Families   Scholastic Professional Books

_ill

ill ill ill ill

Bill
and Jill ...

Jill

25 Read & Write Mini-Books That Teach Word Families   Scholastic Professional Books

Bill

Bill
and Jill
went up the hill
to the mill.

The king
with the ring
likes to sing ...

The
King

sing

ing
ing
ing
ing

3

ring

2

The king
with the ring ...

7

swing

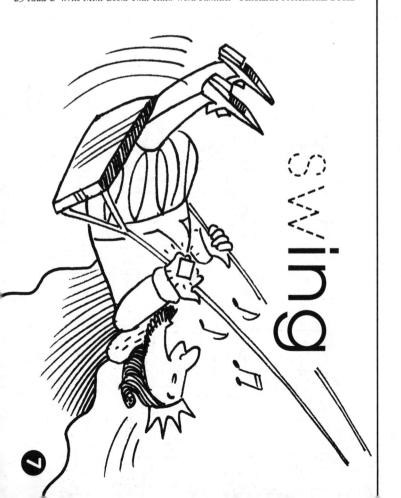

6

The king
with the ring
likes to sing
on his swing.

The peacock
on a rock
heard the clock ...

4

25 Read & Write Mini-Books That Teach Word Families Scholastic Professional Books

c ock

5

The Peacock

____ock

__ock

__ock

tick __ock

8

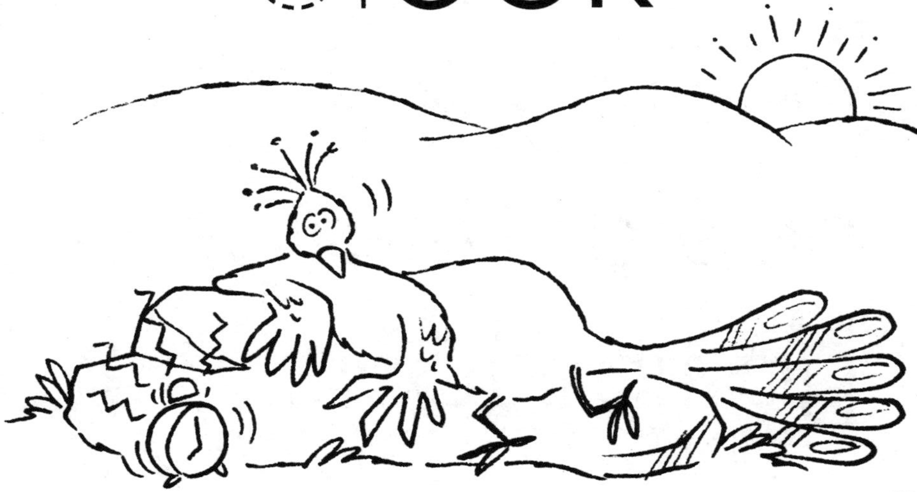

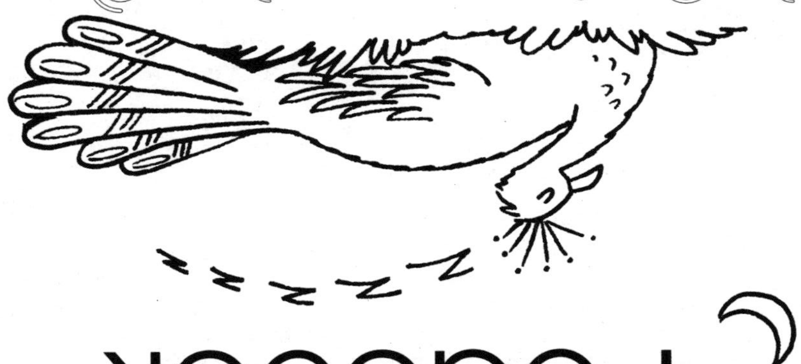

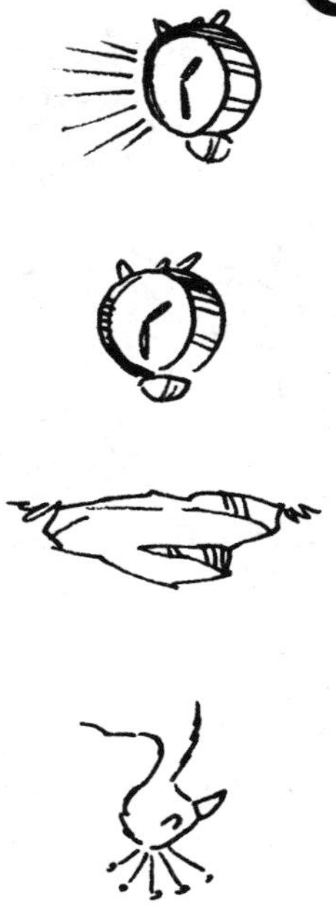

The peacock
on a rock ...

rock

The peacock
on a rock
heard the clock
go tick tock.

tick tock

TICK TOCK

A Frog

_og

_og

_og

__og

8

A frog
and a dog
take a jog ...

4

jog

5

25 Read & Write Mini-Books That Teach Word Families Scholastic Professional Books

A frog
and a dog ...

dog

log

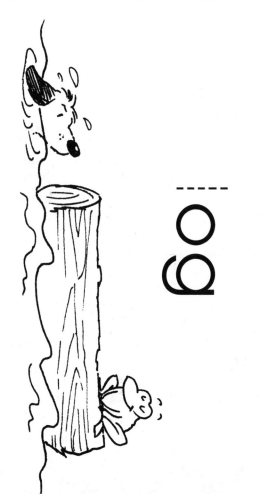

A frog
and a dog
take a jog
on a log.

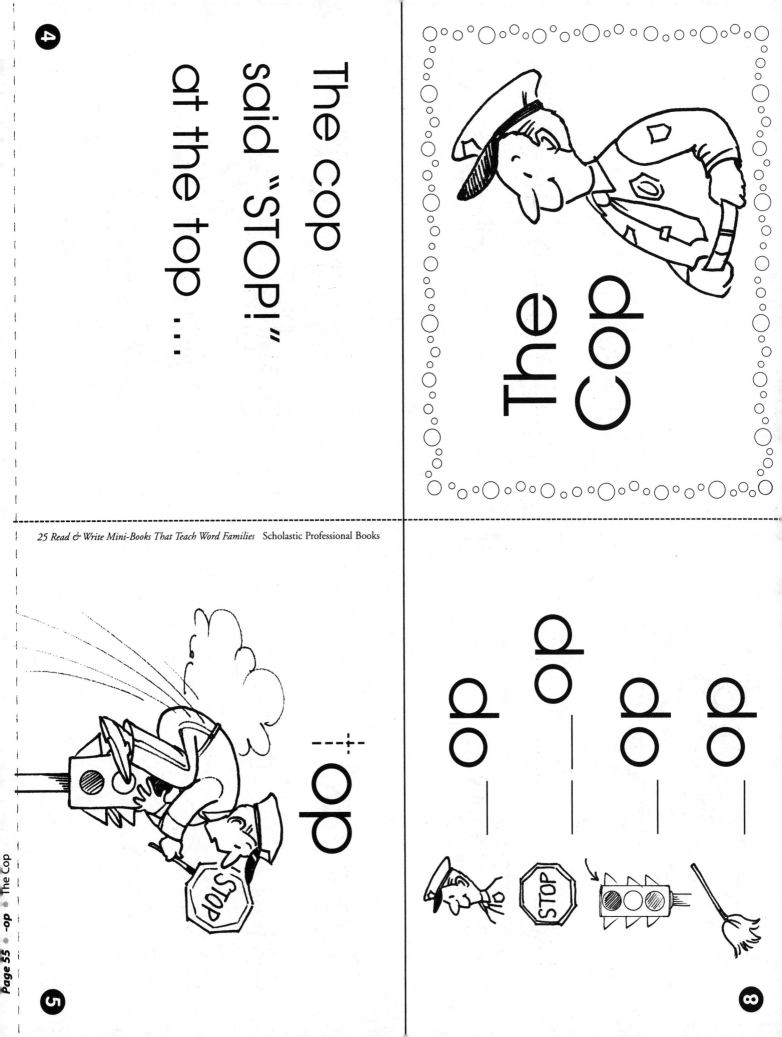

4

The cop
said "STOP!"
at the top ...

The
Cop

25 Read & Write Mini-Books That Teach Word Families Scholastic Professional Books

5

-op

op

op

op op

8

3

st-op

2

The cop
said "STOP!" ...

6

The cop
said "STOP!"
at the top
to a mop.

7

m-op

A cub
has a sub
and a scrub ...

A
Cub

25 Read & Write Mini-Books That Teach Word Families   Scholastic Professional Books

scrub

___ub

___ub   ___ub

___ub

2

A cub
has a sub ...

3

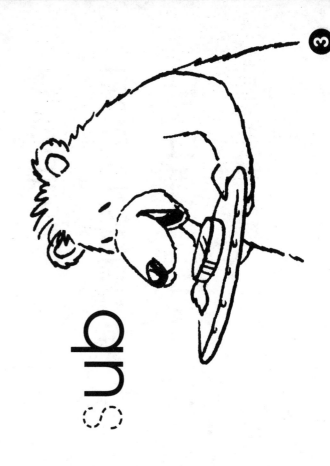

sub

7

tub

6

A cub
has a sub
and a scrub
in the tub.

A bug
on a rug
with a mug ...

25 Read & Write Mini-Books That Teach Word Families   Scholastic Professional Books

mug

ug _____

ug _____

ug _____

ug _____

2

A bug
on a rug ...

3

rug

hug

7

6

A bug
on a rug
with a mug
gets a hug.

4

The skunk
in the trunk
had a bunk ...

The
Skunk

5

bunk

8

unk

_____ unk

_____ unk

_____ unk

The skunk
in the trunk ...

tr unk

j unk

The skunk
in the trunk
had a bunk
filled with junk.